A LOST NEPOLIAN DIARY

NEPOLIAN SERIES

DORIAN SNOWDEN

To my parents,
who taught me the value of
dreams and hard work.

Contents

Contents

Contents

A LOST NEPOLIAN DIARY

DORIAN SNOWDEN

Notion Press Media Pvt Ltd

First Published by Notion Press 2024
Copyright © 2024 Dorian Snowden
All Rights Reserved.
Paperback ISBN-13: 979-8896102762
Hardcover ISBN-13: 979-8896732419

Preface

Travel has a unique way of transforming us, of opening our eyes to the wonders of the world and the depths of our own souls.

'*A Lost Nepolian Diary*' is not just about the destinations, but about the journey itself. It is about the unexpected detours and the quiet moments of introspection that often go unnoticed. Through these pages, I invite you to join me on this journey, to see the world through my eyes, and perhaps to find a piece of yourself in this.

Thank you!

Prologue

Success is more than money and fame. The elegance of living is similar to the grandeur of travelling. Snow-covered caaps of mountains and the adjoining plains that lead to depths of ocean beds create the world of living respect worthy.

It's all about disparity and simplicity that trigger journeying. Often, forgetfulness invites mistakes that become a veil in front of eyes.

Journeying makes footsteps work on to revitalise and fill the soul with miracles of simplistic patterns of living. The window of ignorance opens for many to claim that living is not about failure. But once the wheels start rolling, we get that perspective do the rest.

Dorian Snowden follows the context and declares a new context open. Most of them are paraphrased and logically lined in the book 'A Lost Nepolian Diary' that makes the craze of riding to the world reverberate at regular intervals as one goes on riding. The soliloquies, dialogues, travelogues etc, found in the book share the feel of involvement. The overall impact of reading 'A Lost Nepolian Diary' vitalises the eyes to enjoy the feast of a rich hour in living.

-Godfrey Selvanesan

DISCLAIMER

Don't do motorcycle rides until and unless you and your pillion are properly geared.

Author's Note

The ride took place in 2021, a time when the mask was a mandatory precaution against COVID-19. Therefore, please forgive me for the repeated use of the word 'mask' in this book.
Thank you!

December 18th, 2021

BENGALURU, KARNATAKA

I

4:00

"It's 4 AM!" a female AI voice woke me from my dreamless slumber.

The alarm kept ringing. Like everyone else, I had the tendency to dismiss the alarm and crumble under the blanket because the air was mixed with December cold. With a fifty percent mindset of just-five-more-minutes, I lay there, but the remaining fifty percent forced me to disconnect from my sleep. I sat on the bed, the alarm still ringing and starting to get irritating. As I leaned towards the table to dismiss the alarm, the AI female voice spoke again, **"It's 4:02 AM!"**

I turned off the dim violet illuminating light in the room by dismissing the alarm; a white light dot grabbed my attention. I disconnected and disassembled the laptop charger, placing both the charger and laptop on the bed.

I got freshened up and ready in thirty minutes.

"It's 4:30 AM!" the AI spoke for the last time. I turned it off right away, letting no harm come to anyone. I plugged my phone in to fill the last ten percent of the battery. My packing had already been done the previous night; it was just my laptop, chargers, and blankets that I needed to keep in. I kept them all and went towards my Nepolian, making absolutely no noise. I removed *his* blanket, turned the key and ignition on, and did a few pumps until the sound stopped growling. I went back into the apartment, folded *his* blanket adequately, and kept it inside its cover (which I had washed less than ten hours ago).

I pulled on the rain cover of my rucksack, placed the bag on the pillion seat, placed Nepolian's blanket on top of it, and tied them together on the seat with my bungee cords.

I wanted to knock on the door to say 'bye' to him, but the time was not right for that. The reality that had totally slipped my mind was that I was alone in the apartment; my flatmate had gone for a North-Indian drive the previous morning.

II

4:45

Geared up, I locked the apartment and pushed my Nepolian to the main lane, where it made the least disturbance. I did another couple of pumps with the choke on, and on the third attempt, the bike started.

After idling, I engaged the clutch, pulled to first gear, and as I was about to roll on, I saw a security guard looking at me. I waved bye to him, and he waved back, his smile easily visible in the mild darkness. Then I rolled on. I could see the security guard standing still under the light through my mirror, until I had gone straight for eighty to a hundred meters and took a sharp ninety-degree right turn.

A LOST NEPOLIAN DIARY

III

6:15

The morning was cold and dry. Cruising forty to fifty kilometres per hour was our sweet spot. I always feel good cruising at fuel-efficient speed, enjoying the side scenery in the least human presence. The one thing which always compels me to start the ride in the early mornings is the transmogrification from night to day, that one hour where the sky gets diluted in golden clouds, the birds chit chattering and the radiant emergence of the sun. It's a short time experienceable sight but worth every single second of admiring that transition.

The rising sun rays have some kind of properties, I don't know what exactly that is, all I know is, it's good for health. I pulled over to the side, removed my helmet, and pulled my balaclava in a way so that the rays could touch my face. I have always thought about standing for five to ten minutes to absorb the rays, but haven't got a proper chance yet. Today was also the same, I wanted to reach the halt on time, before night; so I rolled on.

IV

8:15

I reached Mysore, the place where I had mentally planned to have my breakfast. My regular go-to shop was closed, so I went to the next one, which was just ten meters ahead. The shop was half empty, with just a few people having hot beverages.

I ordered one set of idly and a coffee. While I was eating, the owner asked me, "Where are you coming from?"

"Bangalore," I replied.

I was expecting a "Where are you going?" question as well, but instead, he said, "Ride safe!"

"Yes, I will!" I replied with a nod of acceptance.

The tea shop where I was sitting was just three shops beside my regular one. The owner of my regular shop was a Muslim man who always wore a kurta-pyjama and was in his mid-fifties or somewhere near there. A few benches were placed in front of his shop, and there the tea and coffee were served. People usually preferred red tea with their smokes. I had been to the shop more than ten times, and every single time, he would sit in the same spot with a lit cigarette on his left and a black tea on his right. Yes, every single time, that's how I've seen him; all his puffs were the same, long-held in, but the last puffs were different. He took the last puff in, tossed the cigarette into the bin, and exhaled through his nostrils while combing down his long, bulky, chest-level beard. One cigarette for one black tea, that's how he had been doing it for ages. Even though the shop was closed and he wasn't there, I could still picture him on the bench doing the same because that's how I've always seen him, exactly the same.

I sat on Nepolian and checked my WhatsApp to see whether a few of the messages I had sent last night were delivered, but they weren't, just one tick. I called that number, and it said 'switched off,' the same as it had for the past two days. A thought of '*Will the plan get messed up?*' came to my mind.

I checked the time, and it showed 08:47 AM. "There's still time!" I said to myself.

I checked Google Maps and zipped the phone inside the tank bag. I geared up and turned to wave bye to dada (that's what I used to call him), but I totally missed the fact that his shop was closed; habits are like that. Then I rolled on.

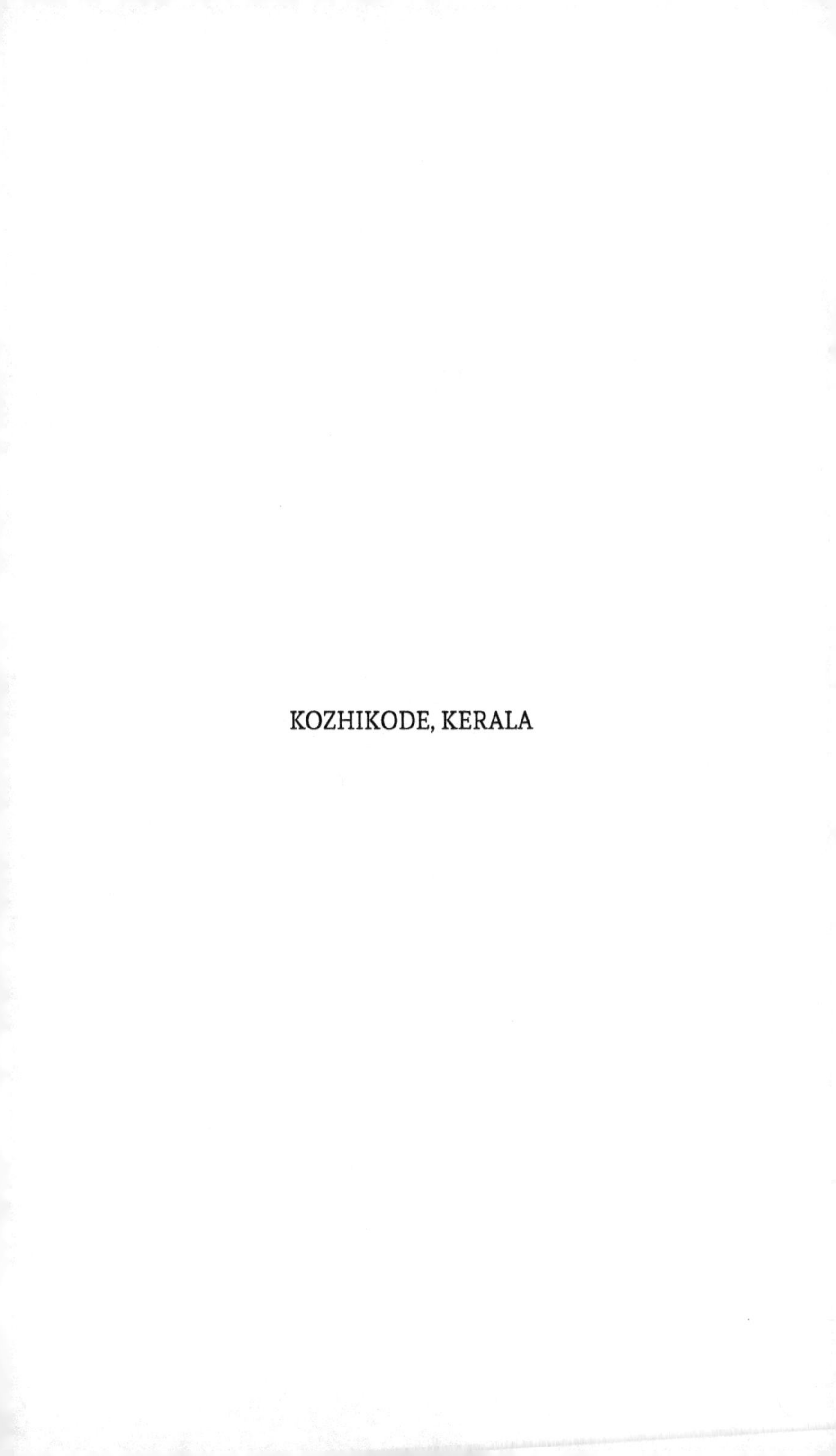

KOZHIKODE, KERALA

V

14:40

With the hot sun above my head and the waving sea to my side, I reached the front of Mahi Church. I pulled over under a tree and did some slight stretching after removing my helmet. The water I carried was finished, and the sun had reduced my body water level. Leaving all my three bags along with my helmet, I went to grab a bottle of water. I always prefer normal water because cold water gives an oozing effect while drinking, but the body has a different story as the chilled water goes in.

I took out my phone from my tank bag and called the number, and it said the same. I checked the WhatsApp message, and the single tick got a companion; it was delivered more than two hours ago but hadn't turned blue. I was confused, so I gulped a few more sips of water, standing under the tree, unsure whether I needed to go or not.

In that bewildered moment, my body was in a circumstantial involuntary activity. Just like our hearing gets sharp after watching a really good horror movie, my nose got sharp as the train in my stomach honked very badly. My eyes automatically blurred, and the smell of salt in the air vanished. I had no clue how my brain did that, but still, it was an abrupt change that I recognized after a while.

With my helmet visor up, I rolled on in search of the delicious-smelling hotel. I passed by a few hotels that smelled of beef roast, beef curry, chicken, and fish varieties, but my brain was commanding one thing, and my stomach was craving the same. My taste buds, well, they were like, 'If it's not that, then we are not going to cooperate with you!' The food was nothing other than 'Thalassery Chicken Biriyani!'

Oh, reader! I'll tell you this, I still feel the saliva rising at the word 'Thalassery Chicken Biriyani'. While I was writing the draft, I stopped at this area because the taste of biriyani hovered on top of my tongue.

'*Yes, I've reached the place,*' I got a gut feeling as I passed by a restaurant. I parked Nepolian at the corner of the restaurant. Just beside where I parked, there was a woman selling fish. I sniffed to check the smell of the fish, but I didn't get it, which I concluded was either my nostrils getting used to the salty air or my brain disabling it for some time.

I got in, took a table in the corner, placed each bag on each chair, upper body armor on the table with the helmet on top, and ordered Thalassery Chicken Biriyani and a lime juice.

VI

To be frank, the quantity was low, smelled appetizing, and tasted good, like, okay-okay (not even close to my expectation), but the lime juice was worth every penny, seriously, so I ordered one more.

I was fine with that biriyani, though not satisfied; it felt to me that something was missing. The dissatisfaction I had was reflected on my face, which made the receptionist ask me directly. Thinking he was just a staff member there, I mentioned my unsatisfactory biriyani encounter while paying.

"One biriyani and two lime juices," I corrected him as he placed the wrong balance on the counter.

"Yes, son!" he replied, closing his drawer.

The multicolor Gandhiji he placed flapped on the counter. He took the balance and handed it to me. He had only charged for the lime juice, not for the biriyani.

"Why?" I asked.

"Customer satisfaction," he replied. The bill was already printed. "Won't they cut your salary?" I asked.

"No, this is my restaurant," he said, with a nod.

I felt awkward because I had just expressed my dissatisfaction straight to the owner himself, and I didn't have anything to say in response. I went numb for a second.

"Actually, our biriyani chef is on leave; he's not well, that's what happened," he said in an apologetic tone.

'*Exactly, everything was there, but the magic factor was missing,*' a thought popped into my head. I gave a smile and a nod to that and left. The restaurant was swamped with takeout orders than dine-in. Through the corner of my eye, I saw the owner looking at me as I was carrying my bag and wearing my jacket. I gave him a wave as I passed in front of him. "Ride safe, son," he wished, waving back.

I sat on my Nepolian with all the bags in their positions. I took my phone to call him again, but the notification showed '**3 missed calls**' from him.

VII

His house was less than ten kilometres from where I was standing. The plot twist was that he wasn't there in his house; he had gone out of state with his family, and the whole house was empty. When he said that, all I could reply was, '*Okay, fine, I'll take a room nearby*' but his reply was, '*You use the outhouse until we reach da*'.

In any unexpected situation like the one I was in, he had already given me a spare key to his outhouse. In the middle of the footpath, I was not at all in the mood to check for the keys in my bags. So I asked whether he had kept any key in his house compound, and the reply was positive.

I reached the front of the house. As he had said, some gardening work was going on there, and due to that, the gate was not padlocked. His house was quite big and had a good area for gardening, which made all the workers stare at me. I stood Nepolian on both legs in the middle of the car porch with all my bags on *him*. I went to ask for the keys, and a gardener guy gave them to me (I was a little lazy to find the keys in my bag, though).

I opened the room, removed my jacket and tossed it on the chair, placed all my bags and helmet on the bed, and sat on the chair. I kept all my things on the bed so that I could sweep the floor and then place them on the floor, but the floor was already clean. Leaving my messenger bag, I kept the other bags on the floor, stretched myself, and placed my jacket on the chair under the rotating fan, my boots on the sides of the door, and my helmet properly under the bed. The floor was clean, so I didn't mind lying on the floor with my riding pants. I lay there for some time to relax my tightened back muscles. The cold from the tiles penetrated me, at first making it unpleasantly cold and then gradually comforting me. The heavy food, rotating fan above me, and peaceful natural environment were heavenly pleasing to me.

Just about to slip into a small nap, the door smashed against the wall, startling me from my peace. "Here," one of the gardeners said, stretching his phone to me.

"Why?" I asked as I stood up, showing all the irritated expressions I knew on my face.

"Sir is calling!" he said, trying to get in and handing me the phone.

'Sir, uh?'

"Hello!" It was my friend who couldn't get through to my phone. As I checked, it was on silent, which is why I didn't hear the rings, and I didn't inform him when I reached or started using his outhouse; so rude of me, wasn't it?

VIII

15:30

After the call, my cat nap's soothing effect evaporated. The sun was indeed at its peak, and calm warm air was breezing rhythmically into the room due to the wide-open door. I had sweated quite a bit on the ride, and standing under the fan, I was thinking about whether I needed to place my jacket out to get some fresh air. I must admit that I was reluctant to do that until I saw some hangers freely dangling on the clothesline. In just a matter of seconds, the hanger waved with my jacket along with my freshly washed balaclava under a shade.

After that, I checked Nepolian for any issues, but *he* was fine, just a bit dusty and slurry on the bottom areas. Not even half an hour had passed with *him* on the car porch, so I didn't check whether *he* was still hot or not because I knew *he* wouldn't be. I went back to the room, took a quick shower, and sorted my things as per my comfort. I lay down for another thirty minutes; that's what I planned, but when I woke up, the time was 05:30 PM. I had slept for more than an hour.

Can't blame myself! I told you the nature vibe was so peaceful and had the least disturbance; I dozed off in that peacefulness.

Due to the distance that I had to cover the following day, I had my dinner around eight thirty p.m. so that I could get to sleep by ten. The table in the room was small, which made it difficult to scatter my things. So I overcame that space issue by sitting on the bed with my things on it.

I wrote down the rough draft of this ride so far. Actually, a whole bundle of my upcoming book was what I checked first; and to be frank, there was literally nothing specific to check for or double-verify or anything of that sort because I had done it all early and was literally ready to be given for typing processes. I kept the bundle of manuscript papers and the rough draft of the book in my messenger bag. My rucksack was fully packed, so I wanted one more bag to keep my manuscripts and my other writing stuff safe and sound and for easy accessibility. 'What if the papers get wrinkled at the corners?' was what haunted me the most.

The struggles of thoughts, the complexity of placing different words to check which one matches properly, trying my best to write in good handwriting, making sure the entire chapter is as per my satisfying level, the thought of conjunctions, running out of words, et cetera, et cetera, all those struggles and frustrations.

In short, the whole process of completing, from a thread to manuscript, feels like a pleasure when I go through those papers. I need to mention, it's a short-term pleasure, but I enjoy it each and every time until the typing starts. (I don't know about other writers).

Over the phone, he said that he would be reaching by evening and insisted me to stay over so that we could meet, but I couldn't make it out that way because around two hundred kilometres is what I wanted to complete the next day, and for that, I needed to wake up early so that I could leave on time. With all my planning for tomorrow and my bags ready to tie up on *him*, I went to bed and rolled under my blanket.

'*Excuse me!*'

"Shit!" Remembering something, I jumped out of bed and turned the light on. I took *his* blanket and wore it properly. I plugged in my phone to charge after checking the alarm, and I turned off the light for the last time of the night.

From apartment to Mahe, Kozhikode

December 19th, 2021

X

Only very few people are fans of waking up with sunrays on their faces, and I'm not one of them. If you ask me how I feel, well, it's one of the most irritating ways to wake up, second only to having water poured on your face.

I stretched myself while lying on bed with the least interest in waking up. The sleep in my eyes was heavy, making it hard to open them, but what could I do? The sunrays were powerful enough to make it impossible to ignore their impact on me. With my eyes squinted, I somehow managed to close the window and flew myself onto the bed. When I say I flew, I seriously flung myself onto the bed; the mattress was so squishy and soft that it absorbed me as I lay on it. I rolled myself under my blanket for another slumber. The brightness in the room was still high, which made me doubt the time. I checked the time on my phone, and it showed 10:05 AM. That was it, no more, no less. I jumped out of the squishy-soft cocoon and started to get ready to leave within the next sixty minutes.

XI

11:30

The route from Vadakara to Kozhikode was a sweaty one. The sun was right above my head, the hot spiky dusty air, traffic, potholed roads, and above all, road widening. Filtering through the traffic and the sudden saves from the potholes were risky, owing to two things: one, the bike was vintage and had its limitations; two, my bags.

I had opened all the vents provided in the jacket for maximum airflow, and I could feel hot air entering, making it warmer inside. Due to the wide handlebars, I could feel the sweat oozing on both my upper sides. My helmet and gloves were the only things that were black in my upper armor, and they had their effects as well. My palms got sticky to the gloves, just like how it feels when we use fruit essence sanitizer a little more than required. The helmet visor was up for air exposure, but it wasn't very helpful due to the boiled air. Even though I could sense that my entire area was soaking wet as hell, there wasn't even a single drop of sweat oozing or dripping on my eyes or my spectacles, and that's the main reason why I prefer a balaclava over a buff.

Buffs are good, cost very little compared to a balaclava, and can be used in many different styles as well, but when it comes to utility under the helmet, I prefer and suggest a balaclava.

XII

_12.00_

In that hot scene, there was some PWD pipe work going on, which made the road narrow and congested, resulting in periodic blocks.

While in one of the last blocks, I saw a tall guy pushing his bike on a steep incline. I wasn't able to understand the issue but deduced it wasn't a puncture. I reached the top of the steep incline and asked him what happened.

"Fuel's over," he replied.

"Where is the nearby pump? I'll get you some petrol," I suggested.

"No thanks," he denied with an open palm gesture. His face was totally sweat-streaming, and he was not wearing a mask. I would have died if I had worn a mask in that situation.

"Bro, I have a small bottle of petrol. You can reach the next petrol pump with that--"

"No need," he said, even without letting me complete, and pointed to a place. "The pump is just near."

"How long have you been pushing the bike?" I asked, looking at his bike and making sure no other passengers were getting into trouble on that narrow road because of us.

"Half a kilometre."

"You can definitely reach there with my bottle. Refill the bottle from there," I replied, looking at the petrol pump, which was less than one-fifty meters ahead.

"It's okay, bro, no need. Thank you for asking!"

"I've been in these situations, so I know the struggle," I replied because I really got into these types of situations and wished for help at that time.

"At least you stopped and asked. That's a big thing, bro."

"No mention."

He offered me a handshake and asked my name.

"Dorian," I replied. "Yours?" I asked, and he replied something, but I wasn't able to hear properly due to the other vehicles.

"Okay then!" I said to him, kickstarting my bike, waving goodbye to the stranger, and rolling on.

Actually, at first, I felt bad because I offered help that he wanted but he denied it. Later it struck me; he did have a rigid point: 'Never accept help from a stranger; you may never know with what intention they are offering it.' That doesn't mean that you should never ever accept any help from strangers, but be aware of the time and occasion, that's it.

If I were in his situation, I would have accepted because, first thing, it's a public area, and after returning his fuel, there is no use for him to be around me. If I feel anything suspicious, then I'll take my phone and make a selfie video clip along with his face, saying 'he helped me in this so-and-so situation' by repeatedly saying his name, place, and vehicle number, and upload it to the family group along with my live location. After this, the chances of getting abducted are minimal.

XIII

It took more time than I expected to get out of the whole sunny narrow path (the PWD work was in a short area, but it had its effect for a long distance, and the national highway widening made the situation worse). The road was not smooth—no potholes, but not proper—which resulted in the slanting of my rucksack. My tank bag was safe; it was a magnetic one, and the metal petrol tank had a wide surface to stick on. So I pulled over to drink and tighten my bag.

I did both, popped my joints, did some basic stretch exercises to relax my back, and waited for another sharp ten minutes for my Nepolian to cool down.

XIV

12:30

Less than fifteen minutes after continuing my ride, I realized someone was following me. I checked through the mirror but wasn't able to recognize him. So I slowed down and waved for him to overtake me. The biker honked as he got parallel to me. I looked at him, and he was the same guy who was pushing the bike. I waved "Hi" and asked, "Have you filled up?"

"Yes, are you in a hurry?" he shouted.

"Not so much. Why? What happened?" I asked, thinking he might need some kind of help or want to take a selfie with me, but instead, he asked, "Shall we have a juice together?"

To be honest, reader, I'm not using any aftermarket sound-amplifying exhaust, but the stock one, and it's comparatively louder than the new generation Enfield1. So due to the exhaust note and the helmet, I wasn't able to hear properly. I asked again by means of a nod and gave a thumbs up to him as a reply.

"You go in front, I will follow you," I shouted and followed him as he went on.

A few hundred meters passed, and I got carried away by a big billboard advertisement while following him. The next thing I saw was his right indicator blinking with his right-hand strength, and he turned to the right from the national highway. Looking through the mirror, I made sure no vehicles were right behind me; two downshifts along with front and rear brakes simultaneously with the indicator to the right, and I followed him with a slight skid, but no harm to anyone2.

XV

12:40

Call me old-fashioned, I don't care; I hate to park bikes under the sun. I always want a shaded place to park. The place he took me to was crowded, and by that sight, I understood the shop is well known for what they provide. It wasn't a struggle to find a shade there. By the time I parked and removed my helmet, balaclava, and gloves, he had ordered and came back with two cups.

The shop was indeed crowded, so I wore my sling bag because it had my baby in it. The shop was on the left of the road, and to the right was a pond, a really massive pond that apparently belonged to a temple.

We stood slightly away from the crowd, and I placed my cup on the table. "How much for this?" I asked, pulling out my wallet.

"I paid, bro," he said, taking a sip.

"Yeah, how much for both?" I asked, looking for an orange Gandhiji in it.

"Don't offend me, bro," he replied in a pale, monotone voice.

'*What kind of reply was that?*' I thought. "Okay," I replied with a shrug and tucked in the wallet.

He was tall, around six feet two inches to six feet three inches, with short hair and a four-day stubble, carrying a small side bag like mine. "What do you do?" I asked, noticing the black marks on his knuckles.

"Completed my +2, now doing chartered accountancy."

"Oh-kay."

"And what's your name, by the way?" he asked abruptly.

"Dorian Snowden!"

He looked at me from top to bottom.

I burst out into laughter at his smirked look.

"Is that your real name?"

"Yeah, bro!"

"Such a unique name."

"Thank you!"

"So! Solo ride?" he asked.

"Yeah."

"Where are you heading?"

"Dead south!" I replied, taking a big gulp of the sapota juice.

"And from where did you start?"

"Bangalore."

"So you will be reaching 'dead south' today itself?"

"No."

The jacket made me uncomfortable. I wanted to remove it and place it somewhere or hang it up, but I couldn't, so I unzipped it fully. "I'm staying in Alappuzha tonight, and from there, it depends on a few calls."

"Mhm..." he grunted, stirring his cup. "So what do you do?"

"I'm a writer," I replied.

"So you are a writer!" he said, looking again from top to bottom.

"Yeah."

"But you don't look like a writer," he replied in confusion.

A few seconds of silence passed by, me enjoying the pond and the cold fresh juice in my hand.

"How long had you been pushing your bike?" I asked.

"Half a kilometre or something, but no one asked for help other than you, bro."

"Been there, so I know the struggle," I said with a grunt. "You haven't said your name yet!" I complained.

"Akshay!" he said.

"Dor--"

"Dorian!" he replied.

"Wow!" I was impressed. "Usually, people tend to forget my name so easily."

"My mind is very sharp," he replied, tipping his index finger to his sideburns.

"I appreciate that," I complimented.

"I have never met a writer before," he said and offered me a handshake.

"Ooh! Now you have," I said, smiling at his words and accepting his handshake.

XVI

12:45

The breeze from the pond was warm. The ripples being formed were worth watching—a large pond with no plastic waste or any plants anywhere in it, a totally plain, clean, fresh-looking pond. The way the wind made the ripples from the far side of the spectator was worth watching along with the cold fresh juice.

I can openly say this: people may or may not observe this, but the pond view is what makes the juice experience more soothing.

Our chat went on. "Do you know what a manuscript is?" I asked.

"No."

"Wanna see one?" I asked with a smile.

"Bro, I won't be able to understand anything. I'm doing chartered accountancy."

"Okay!"

"So what is your manuscript about?"

"It's a travelogue."

"How long did it take you to reach the manuscript?"

"Actually--"

"So you write about travelling?" he asked, with his eyes wide open.

"Not 'only' travelling," I said, making a quote gesture.

"Okay!" he wiped his mouth. "How many travelogues have you written so far?"

"All set to publish my first travelogue on this 25th."

"So you have your second travelogue work with you?"

"Yeah," I smiled.

"Now, what all things do you have to do after the manuscript phase?" he asked.

"It needs to be typed in and then edited, that's all."

"So in a month, will this book be ready to publish?"

"Typing itself will take more than two weeks--" his curiosity made him eager, making it hard to complete my sentence.

"Editing time?"

"More than six months--"

"This is the first time I've heard about a manuscript, so just curious."

"Can understand," I said with a side nod.

Nodding, he tossed his empty cup into the bin.

"Anyway, bro, I need to reach Kozhikode early."

"Yeah, sure."

"It was nice to meet you!" he gave his last handshake and walked towards his bike. Tossing my cup into the bin, I walked towards Nepolian. By the time I wore my balaclava, he took a U-turn and left with a waving hand. I took another few minutes to gear up and joined the national highway to continue my ride.

13:05

An average of fifty kilometres might have passed, and my bike went to reserve. I knew I would get another sixty to seventy kilometres in reserve, not like what happened in *'Finally on my Nepolian'*.

The sun was freaking hot, and I wanted to pull over. I found a petrol pump that had the things I always looked for: a large area and grass with shade on the side, where I could sit and relax.

I fueled up for six eighty rupees, and the cost for one litre was one hundred four rupees and sixty paise. I pushed Nepolian to one side so that no other vehicles would be inconvenienced by mine. I stood *him* on both legs, and except for my riding pants, I removed all my armour. I did my usual routine—cracking my joints, doing small stretch exercises, and splashing water onto my face.

Every time I go for long rides (over three hundred kilometres) on my Nepolian, I always carry a hundred-millilitre small bottle of engine oil with me. Each time before I refill in between the rides, I pour ten millilitres of engine oil into the tank, and this improves the riding experience (mine has a carburetor, and this is only suitable for carburetor, not fuel injection models). I sat and relaxed so that the engine could cool down. Meanwhile, a white guy, five feet eight inches with a noticeable tummy, came to me, and the first question he asked was, "By any chance, are you selling this?"

As usual, my reply was rapid-fire, "No, not at all."

He looked around my bike and said, "I also tried a number plate like this, but I didn't get this look. It stuck out on my bike."

"Which model do you own?" I asked.

"New model."

"That's why!" I commented.

"I tried to make mine look like this, but it didn't work out."

"Ooh!" I felt sorry for him.

Reader, if you are thinking what is special about the number plate, it's placed on the mudguard. 'Flag type' is what that model is known as, and what makes it more appealing is the beading on the mudguard.

"Do you get proper brakes with this?" he asked in a reasonable manner.

I went numb. I mean, seriously, most people just looked at it and left, but he asked. Only enthusiastic people asked that. Seeing me bewildered, he asked, "It provides poor braking, right?"

"Yes, it's cycle-hub, and the braking feedback is not that great," I said, sharing my honest experience.

"In case of emergency, what will you do?"

"Engine braking!"

"Will get stopped with engine braking?"

"Forty-fifty is my max speed, so in that range, it's fine."

"Okay-okay!" he nodded.

"If you are using the latest brakes and use this, then it might get you in trouble," I completed.

"Can't rely on these brakes,"

"Yes, you can't," I admitted.

"Which model is this?" he asked, looking at the old registration.

"This is an early 1982 model."

"I thought you might say 'Yes, I am selling this'."

"Naa," I grinned.

"It's hard to maintain, though!" he complained.

"Yes, it is," I admitted, "but for me, it's worth it. I get satisfaction while riding on it, so I'm not complaining about anything."

He nodded, looking at Nepolian.

"Did you own one before?" I asked because the way he looked at the bike made me feel like he had one.

"No, no... I wanted to, but it's hard to maintain, so I took a new one."

"Emmm," I sighed.

'Evident that you are regretting now,' I thought.

"Solo ride?" he asked, tapping on the rucksack.

"Yeah."

"Ride safe, buddy!" he wished, and with a handshake, he left with a few turn-back looks at my Nepolian.

This is not the first time I have received compliments or people coming near and asking about Nepolian, but I feel good every time because there are literally people who appreciate old-school bikes. There are some scenarios where I receive doubtful comments like 'Doesn't this have a self-start?', 'Why does your bullet look weirder than the other Bullet?', 'How much did you pay for this type of registration number?', "What is this lever above the gear lever?" and so on and so forth.

The sun helped me in a good way that I realized after emptying my bottle to half. All I had to do was drink water, and there was no need to go to the toilet to excrete it; the sun sucked the water. Yes! Sounds silly, but the day was diabolically hot.

XVIII

19:00

Just a few dozen kilometres before Kochi, I took a small rest at one of the petrol pumps; actually, I got an important call, and for that, I pulled over. The road wasn't smooth, so the path wasn't enjoyable. As I'd mentioned earlier, I looked for certain things before entering, and the grass area was what impressed me there. The wide grass was soft, so I laid on it.

I had a bad experience once; it was in Chennai, I couldn't recollect which pump it was. I was lying on the grass freely, and one of the staff came over to me and asked if I was okay health-wise, but it wasn't like that. He made an unwanted scene, which resulted in the manager ending it, and after that experience, I asked before resting. Nevertheless, no one had said 'No!' so far.

Here, I didn't ask them. I entered, stood *him* on both legs, and removed my helmet. I continued the call, realized the grass was soft, removed my jacket, and laid down after finishing the call. As I started enjoying the relaxation, I felt a needle penetrating my face and biceps at the same instance. I sat still, wore my spectacles, and found the mosquitoes. They were humongous, measuring one centimetre long; if you are wondering how I was so sure, I literally took one of the mosquitoes I killed and measured it later.

I drank water and realized that if the mosquitoes hadn't been there, I would have laid there ignoring the existence of time. I'm not exaggerating; the grass was soft. While I was armoring up, I heard shouting on the other side of the road. I saw fire hovering in mid-air, BJP flags flapping, and a protest going on. I had no clue what it was for, literally no idea at all. The road got blocked by them, and what surprised me was the strength. Even if I took some rough count, it could have definitely been two-fifty to three hundred people in that protest. A few wore masks, a few didn't, and the rest wore them covering just their chin (for namesake).

By that sight, I didn't doubt if the Omicron variant would spread quickly in that area. I was not aware of the reason for the protest, so I don't have any right to judge their protest. I waited for a while until they left the national highway and the block dissolved, and I continued the ride.

XIX

Ayoor to Ernakulam District Bridge.

20:48

On this bridge, I took another twenty-minute break. I got down, removed my helmet, and kept it on the footpath while I looked at the river beneath me.

The water looked pitch dark, and the only distinguishable feature was the white dot on the wobbling river—the moon. A few other tiny lights illuminated the banks of the river, but other than that, it was, as I said, pitch black. Not to mention other vehicles passing by with honking. The bridge was a 'one-way' lane, but I pulled over there with maximum effort not to cause any difficulty to anyone. I turned the lights and the indicator on for maximum visibility, not the hazard light, just the left indicator.

So here is the thing! I do promote the use of hazard lights on bikes because they have their own purpose, but turning them on the road just for show-off is not their only use. If the bike is parked on the side of the road with the person on it; a sudden trouble situation on the road in front of you and you want to indicate behind you; you are facing some issue with your bike and want to indicate to other vehicles and ask for help from other vehicles—these are the main scenarios where the hazard light comes into play. But nowadays, people, especially youngsters, use it as a purpose of show-off. And I don't understand the use of forty to sixty types of blinking patterns in hazard lights.

See! The hazard light has a functional purpose, not a fancy light decoration for the bike. When people misuse features like these, the people who use them for the purpose won't be able to convey the message properly.

I wanted to install the hazard lights, but the problem was that I wasn't able to place the switch within finger reach. There is no slot for switches on the right socket. The only switch there is the kill switch, which too wasn't there on Nepolian when it was manufactured. The other place where I could assemble the switch was on the handlebar, and that's a no-no for me for two reasons.

1. The purpose of it on the road is immediate, and if it is not within finger reach, the caution-there-is-a-problem-on-road-ahead signal will be lagged. Imagine taking your hand from the handlebar, turning it on, and then holding the handle back. This consumes time. This is why companies are placing the switch within finger reach, just like the kill switch.
2. I don't want to ruin the vintage look of my Nepolian, the look that I don't want to be diluted; the look that I have been maintaining and taking care of for ages.

I stood on the bridge for some time and took some pictures and videos, but to no avail; I wasn't able to capture what I saw with my four eyes. The footpath was about two feet higher than the road, and that troubled me to hop on *him*. I placed myself safely between the bags and rolled on with my visor up.

ALAPPUZHA, KERALA

XX

'Call me as soon as you reach Cherthala railway station!' was the audio reply I got for my *'send me your location'* WhatsApp text message.

This Cherthala railway station was on the roadside of National Highway 66, which made it easier for me, but no one told me on which side of the road it was. There was a huge tree that I had marked for the station, a landmark; and at night, I couldn't see that. I was not absent-minded. I was just overconfident in finding the tree, which made the railway station skip from my eyes.

My friend's timing was impressive because he called as soon as I asked an auto driver, 'Where is the railway station?' and he pointed to my rear side. I could see the station board from where I stood. The railway station was empty, which is why it didn't stand out to me at first glance.

The only thing that my friend said on the phone was, 'Just come ten kilometres straight from the railway station, and you will see me.'

And I rode on.

XXI

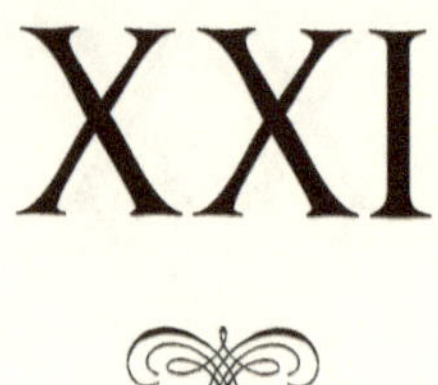

21:30

The time would be around nine thirty p.m. The rush on
the road was almost nil, no transport buses or other heavy
vehicles, just a few cars that passed one or two in a while at
three-digit speed, resulting in the solitude that I preferred.
The small roadside shops were closed. The street light on
the empty footpaths made me feel lonely, just like the
footpath. The trees on both sides were motionless and
provided a feeling of safety to my body and soul, and the
slight cold in the air changed my well-being. Surprisingly,
the road didn't have potholes, which resulted in butter
smoothness from Nepolian. My mind and body relaxed, and
I just hovered on *him*.

Take my words! I was just sitting on the bike and
relaxing, enjoying the feeling, and it was Nepolian who took
charge. I was in a trance of unloading all the tiredness and
sweaty feeling that I encountered from the sun; but on top
of all, I was enjoying the whole ten kilometres at its best.
Hovering at forty kilometres per hour on the silent national
highway, with my Nepolian's dhup-dhup-dhup emitted

from a heavy cranked engine, was a symphony to me, an old school boy.

So far, in every ride I have done—every single ride—there is that one scenario where Nepolian made me feel why it is perfectly okay to escape from the misery of stressful life for a few days and connect with oneself. I could feel the inner side of me rejuvenating as the wind got into my helmet. The night was cold in a comfortable manner. I enjoyed every metre riding on my Nepolian!

22:00

"Britto!" I heard him calling me (Some people have a hard time pronouncing my name properly at the initial stages, so they come up with names they are comfortable with, and 'Britto' was his). He waved at me from the other side of the highway. If he hadn't called me, I swear I would have been going in that auto-pilot mode.

In another ten minutes, I reached his house. On the way, he asked me a few things, but the exhaust and my helmet didn't compromise, so he repeated them all as we parked our bikes.

"No one is here now. They will all reach only after twelve, so sleep off after dinner, or else you won't be able to," he said with a wink.

The next fifteen minutes were at jet speed. I took a shower, bubbled and flowed all the Delta, Delta plus, Omicron, and what-all-variants-that-God-knows into the septic tank. I had my dinner with him, made a few phone calls, and laid on the bed with the lights off for my mental, physical, and emotional recharge.

XXIII

3:30

A strong thought whipped me out of my sleep; it was painful. I jumped out of bed, searched for the light switch, and turned it on. I remembered placing my rucksack and tank bag in the room but not my messenger bag. I searched the entire room but couldn't find it. I went to Nepolian to check whether I had placed it anywhere near *him*, but the outcome was negative. I went mentally numb at that time. I didn't know what to do. I tried to remember where it might have gone, but my head got clouded, my heartbeat raised, and my body started to sweat in that span of time.

My heart ached in my chest. I was in the grip of my involuntary actions. I was sure that the bag was nowhere near me, and my hope diminished.

I lost my bag, I lost my manuscript, and my brain and heart admitted the fact. I wanted to scream out loud but realized I was getting weak. I didn't have any hope of finding it as well. The last time I remember properly was when I was with Akshay (the bike-pushing guy in Kozhikode), and after that, I had covered four to five districts; even worse, I had stopped at a few petrol pumps, a few tea shops, and even on roadsides for no particular reason at all.

When I was on the Thrissur-Kochi national highway, I saw a bike garage that was restoring one of my all-time favourite bikes. I had a long chat with the mechanic and took a few pictures of the bike he was working on. I checked those pictures, and all I could see was my helmet and my gloves in those pictures, not my bag in sight. From that, I concluded two things: either I lost it at the juice place, or I had lost it somewhere else. Anyway, I had lost it, and even if I had all my good luck with me, I doubted I would get it back!

Drops of pain rolled down my sweaty face.

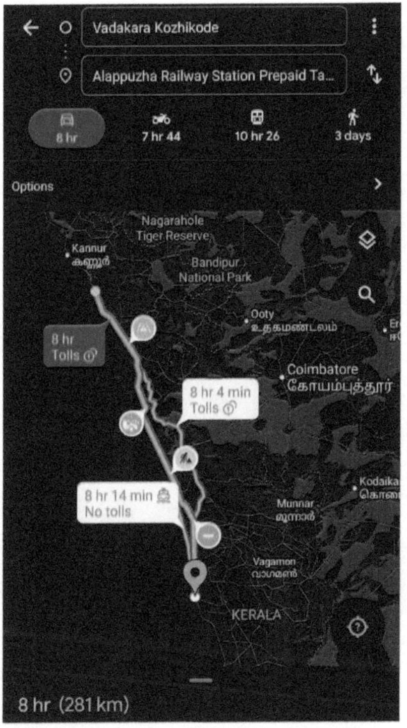

From Kozhikode to Alappuzha

December 20th, 2021

XXIV

I didn't sleep the rest of the night. The realization of 'losing the manuscript' caused insomnia. Everything was in that bag—the thread, rough draft, first draft, manuscript; literally everything, and now I don't have the time or patience to write it all again.

I called the juice parlour at around ten a.m., hoping that they had found a bag and kept it safe with them, but they didn't get anything. I mentioned the physical features of the bag so that he could recollect something, but it was negative. He understood the importance of the bag to me. He tried to comfort me by saying he would definitely reach out if someone handed it over to him. But deep down, I knew the chances were low for that kind of outcome.

To be frank, there were a few incidents that I enjoyed writing down. Seriously, I loved and was pleased to write those parts, but no use, I lost it.

XXV

Evening

I held the melancholy within me, spent the whole day suppressing it, and talked with everyone. But at the end of the evening, Ashokan asked me, "Are you alright?"

"Yeah, a bit tired of riding," I lied.

There was a temple celebration that we talked about in the morning, and Ashokan said he was going to watch it along with his friends. I was not at all inclined towards his insistence.

XXVI

19:30

The time showed 07:30 PM on my phone, and the thoughts in my head doubled and tripled. Losing my bag wasn't the only thing; a few other things were also messing with my head, and due to that, I felt the pressure increasing as the minutes passed by. 'It's always better to deviate our thoughts when we are facing a rough time,' I knew it, but until Ashokan said this dialogue to me, I wasn't ready to leave his house compound. Understanding my disturbed state of mind, he avoided all his friends. He, his brother-in-law, and I went to the temple.

XXVII

A piece of fact that I missed from the chat was that the festivals were taking place in two temples, and I merged them both and thought it was one.

We went to the first temple—nothing much significant to be explained there. The temple was on the main road with village greenery, a pre-smartphone era feel in every aspect, the same ditto scenes shown in old movies.

The temple was crowded, and the current festival that was taking place was not the main big festival. Due to that, the oil lamps on the metal stands that had been placed weren't lit. The lack of proper lights was what made the picture of the temple not found in the book (I could have taken the picture in the morning, but the beauty lacked in daylight).

We sat on the sand for some time, and Ashokan started to tell the history and other stories and beliefs of the temple, but none of the things went into my head. Physically, I was there, but mentally, I was lost.

XXVIII

On our way to the second temple, a word from him shocked me. I triple-checked what he had said. I stopped Nepolian and made him repeat what he said. An honest smile emerged on my face, and no one saw that because of the mask, which was mandatory in the area.

We entered the sub-road that had the temple arch. Both sides towards the temple were packed with bikes, so Nepolian entered the temple premises with no pillion. Ashokan spotted a spot; I made *him* stand on both legs. Since the land was sand, *he* dangled freely on *his* legs as I made *him* to. It took some time to find a long rock from there and place it under *his* legs. *He* stood rooted solid. I locked my helmet on *him* and mingled into the crowd to see the main attraction that I went for. I asked Ashokan where it was because he said there were five of them.

Reader! I insist you believe that I'm not obsessed with it, but if I get a chance to be near it, there is no doubt that I'm going to abnegate that.

Seeing me curiously looking for it, Ashokan took me to one side of the temple where he knew it wouldn't be, just to tease me, because he understood that I came to see them. He even started to use the word to increase my impatience, and he did succeed. By the way, they are humongous, black, strong, beautiful, rough and tough-looking but childish when loved: the elephants.

If you ask me what's there to admire about elephants or say they are not childish, my reply is that you haven't been friends with an elephant. Yes, seriously, you haven't. I know that's not a common thing, so acknowledge your lack in that. Elephants are really good living beings with morals in their lives. They are helping, caring, kind, and not selfish creatures when compared with humans.

I saw the first one under a coconut tree, fully groomed with all the religious decorative items. I went closer, leaving Ashokan (actually, the place was crowded, so I thought he might have left me there and gone somewhere else). I stood beside the elephant and looked at it. There were no proper visible lights hitting the elephant. I tapped on its left tusk, and it oscillated its trunk and flapped its ears. If you are thinking how I came to know that elephant was 'he,' it's simple: by its head and trunk. The easiest way to recognize it is by looking at an elephant's underbelly, but I feel that's being a pervert. I took my hands on him as he raised his trunk. He placed his trunk on the place where I tapped, and I tapped on his trunk. I'm not stupid enough not to know that my touch won't feel much on him, but he liked it. He was older, maybe around twenty-five to thirty plus.

I looked at others around me because they were staring at me in discomfort. Due to me, they weren't able to take pictures with the elephant because the abrupt trunk rise made everyone think twice, and one guy even told me to move so that he could take a proper selfie.

I lost my balance as Ashokan pulled me from behind. Owing to the sand, I tipped over.

"Don't go near it," he warned.

"Why?"

"What if it loses its mind and kills you?"

'*Okay! That's logical,*' I thought.

"It's always safe to stay away from elephants. At least you will get time to run for your life," he said with a touch of humour.

Dusting away the sand from my back, I nodded 'yes.' He pulled me away from the crowd, and we sat under another tree, waiting for all the five elephants to get lined up.

XXIX

20:00

Honestly, I don't have much interest in spending time with elephants that are in festivals. Because they are under the control of the mahout, but the story is different when they are in their homely place. They will be friendly (not all elephants are friendly though; once you get emotionally closer, then you can explore their childish dimension).

Sitting under the tree, I looked at everyone around me and felt like an outdated guy when everyone was busy with their smartphones, and I was wondering 'where I kept my phone'. I didn't quite remember when I gave it to Ashokan, but he gave it to me. I made a call, and it ended up unattended. I felt odd about that. Instead of calling again, I waited, tucked my phone into my pocket, and forced him to accompany me to see the other four elephants. I was a little insecure about my dress code when the majority of the people were wearing mundu, and I was in my blue denim, but when I saw the main crowded area, I got plenty of company, and the mask mandate was almost nil.

See, if you ask me what's there to see in elephants in that decorated state, frankly, I don't know. The elephants are decorated as a part of religious beliefs, so it's comprehending for me to admire. If you are not from the southern side of India, you may not have heard about 'Thrissur Pooram,' and that's a massive festival. I've never been there, even though I got chances to. I have a solid reason for not attending, i.e., 'I won't be able to be with elephants in their friendly, childish state of mind, before and after the Pooram.' Before the Pooram, they would be getting ready for the packed festival, and after the Pooram, they would be tired. Another reason is that I like to be near them when people are least (in single digits).

XXX

20:30

The time had come for all the elephants to stand side by side, and the rumble of chains from each corner was audible. Out of nowhere, Ashokan's brother-in-law pulled my hand and took me to the other side. Until that very moment, I had forgotten he also came with us. We three stood in the front row to see the rowed-up elephants. The one who said to stay away from elephants was the one making space for me. By this far, you might have thought that I was obsessed with elephants, didn't you? In fact, I am not like *that*. I am just a guy who found out that they are not as solid, rough, and tough as they look. I took a small video of all five elephants with two people each on top with decorative umbrellas and other items. That was a colourful sight, and the chenda melam was vibing. As I've said, I was not a fan of seeing elephants in these scenarios, so I passed from the so-called capturing-the-moment people. I sat under a tree and listened to the chenda melam.

XXXI

The rest of the night in his house wasn't for me. A few of his friends came over and were having a serious talk. I wanted to sit alone and focus on my mental health, but I understood it was just making it even worse. So I spent a long time talking with his elder sister, Sethu, who was around forty and had crystal-clear knowledge of Hindu mythology. Till the last strand of my capability of tiredness, I listened to Ramayana stories, and I slept off totally forgetting to wear *his* blanket, my Nepolian.

December 21st, 2021

XXXII

10:45

Waving bye to everyone in Ashokan's house, I left. I wanted to join National Highway 66, where I would be cruising the rest of the day. The route from his house to the national highway was not clear to me, so he joined me until National Highway 66. Since Nepolian is old, he doesn't have any Trip 1 or Trip 2 technical specifications. Either you have to remember (that's what the majority of old-school bike owners used to do) or write them down. So, I took a picture and kept the phone in the side compartment of my tank bag, unzipped.

A maximum of ten kilometres might have been covered on the national highway when I realized that my speedometer was possessed. It was showing its own readings, which was far better than a puncture. I pulled over to the Royal Enfield mechanic on the highway side, and he couldn't fix it because the speedometer cable he had was short (cable for front-wheel assembly).

This may sound weird to many of you readers. In olden bikes, the speedometer dome was attached to the rear wheel, and later the company found out it was more reliable to have the speedometer set up on the front wheel. A few of my mechanics suggested changing the setup to the front wheel, but I was not willing to ruin the manufactured system *he* had.

With a broken speedometer, I rolled on, searching for a Royal Enfield spare parts store, and I found one beside the showroom on the national highway roadside.

XXXIII

A female staff member was at the counter. I asked for the cable, and she gave an expression of do-you-know-what-you-are-asking. I repeated, but she was not at all willing to admit that the speedometer set was assembled on the rear wheel, and she argued with me, saying, 'The speedometer dome doesn't come in the rear wheel,' not to mention I used the term 'old model' properly and repeatedly.

Her attitude in which she spoke made me doubt whether her family used to manufacture Royal Enfield motorcycles in her basement.

"Is there any male staff here?" I asked when another female staff member asked about the issue. A white guy came from inside and said he wanted to see the setup. He looked at it seriously, with both hands on his hips, and asked, "Any plan on selling this?" I burst into laughter; all the after-effects of pointless awkward arguments with that dumb female staff member evaporated instantly. "No, no, I'm not," I replied with a tap on his shoulder.

"Yeah, I know that. It's actually people who don't know much about these old schools who sell them."

"Maintenance is a key factor."

"Yeah," he nodded. "Sir! You do one thing: take a U-turn from the signal and take the first left. Just before a hundred metres on the right, you'll see a Maruthi showroom, and just opposite that, a small way in, there you will find an old-school mechanic," he said, gesturing.

"Thanks, and for the cable?" I asked.

"You will get it there, sir."

"Okay."

"Yes, sir!"

"And one more thing," I said as he was about to walk back.

"What, sir?"

"If possible, tell her that if she doesn't know about something, admit that, instead of wasting others' time."

He grinned with a how-will-I-say-that-sir look.

"Happy ride, sir!" he wished as he walked back to the showroom.

I didn't want to yell back, so I gave a nod and a thumbs up as he looked over his shoulder.

XXXIV

11:30

It took ten minutes to reach the garage due to traffic. I waited another fifteen minutes for the mechanic.

I removed all the bags and placed them on another Enfield, which didn't have an engine. I placed both my bags together. While waiting for him, I thought and was amazed to realize how absent-minded I was. The smallest and most important among all, which I hung on me because of the fear of losing it. I should've placed the bag like that itself in my rucksack, but what changed my mind was the bungee cords. They were tied tightly, and it led to dents and wrinkles in the bag, resulting in the impact on the papers as well. I kept on cursing myself till the mechanic reached.

The mechanic diagnosed the problem, and it was with the speedometer dome, not the cable. It took around thirty to forty-five minutes to solve it. He removed the headlight, unlocked the chain, removed the exhaust, removed the tire, and then changed the dome. This was indeed a tiresome and irritating task, and if the dome was on the front wheel like the latest version, it would have taken less than half the time.

The mechanic also suggested assembling the dome to the front wheel for easy accessibility and reliability to the speedometer cable4.

The sun had entered its peak, and the vents on my gear did their job but weren't very helpful. I went on trying to find a really good parking (shade) available hotel. The national highway was where I needed to be rolling on to reach my next halt, and I was on the right path; all I had to do was ride two hundred kilometres straight on the national highway, which wasn't very interesting due to the immense heat. But I recognized something strange, a slight change in something that reflected the overall well-being of Nepolian. *His* sound had changed; now *he* sounded royal, bold, and aggressive compared to before. Well, now it is what it is, and I liked that new exhaust note. So I rolled on in the fifty to sixty-five kilometre per hour comfort cruising zone, enjoying his new dup-dup-dup.

XXXV

'*So what's next?*'

'I don't know,' I replied.

'*Hmm.*'

'Wait! Regarding what?' I asked.

'*Our lost book, A Nepolian Adventure!*'

I exhaled deeply. 'No idea, but no patience to write that again though.'

'*We lost everything, right?*'

'Yes.'

'*Even the thread?*'

'I do remember all of it, but I don't have much patience to write again or have another few months to spend on it,' I replied.

'*Yes, other things are pending!*'

'Exactly!' I admitted.

'*What is lost is lost, try to be more cautious!*'

'Aah! Not gonna carry that separately!'

'*An unforgettable lifelong experience!*'

'Yep!' I replied to myself with a grunt.

XXXVI

As I said earlier, it's just two hundred kilometres straight on National Highway 66, and I knew the route pretty well, so checking Google Maps wasn't necessary for me. Just like many riders, I also prefer not to put my phone in my armour but rather on the tank bag, and this caused me to miss all of Christo's calls. I saw his missed calls at the fuel stop and called back right away, and my stay for that night got arranged. He had given me his house gate key way earlier.

The road was okay-okay—not too much traffic or rush. Everything was fine except the sun, which was penetrating badly in some places. I sincerely felt like the air getting in was what made me sweat, and that turned out to be true.

XXXVII

The sun's intensity reduced the water not only in me but also in my bottle. I got thirsty and tired due to the heat. So I pulled over to the next tender coconut vendor and drank one. I sat on the raised concrete pavement under the tree for some time with my jacket removed. I felt lighter, and the air flowed over me, giving me a touch of relaxation. When it went into my hair, waving my hair made me feel like a cold water drop sliding over my scalp. I sat for a while, checking whether any sunray was hitting on *him*. I was tired due to the extreme heat because I even had a mindset of taking a cat nap there but wasn't able to. The bumpy road had misplaced my bags, so I adjusted them to their proper positions and sat again in the same spot on the concrete. I haven't taken naps on the roadside or in bus stops in the middle of my rides so far. But I didn't have a yoga mat with me, or else I could have taken a small nap over there. The banyan tree was big enough to provide a large shade, and the coconut guy felt pity seeing my red drunken-like eyes owing to dust.

Actually, it's a personal preference. If you are a person who doesn't care what others think and want to lower the tiredness, then the yoga mat is good. And yes, people will say some things about that, but who cares—'I know how much I'm tired, and I don't want anyone to suffer because of my one-second absent-mindedness due to tiredness.'

I filled my bottle with tender coconut and placed it in my bag. I always wanted to own a hydration bag because it was both properly organized and easily accessible compared to drinking from a bottle, but I couldn't own one. When I wanted to buy, there wouldn't be sufficient Gandhiji with me, and when I had Gandhiji, I would have already ordered something, totally forgetting the hydration bag from my wishlist and smiling like an idiot when the hydration bags showed in the 'recently searched items' list.

Since I sat under the tree for some time, I was ready to start again but felt like drinking one more and sitting for a while. The ten-minute break that I gave *him* after every eighty to one hundred kilometres was over, but I decided to give a few minutes more, trying to suppress and deviate myself from the lost work thoughts.

THIRUVANANTHAPURAM, KERALA

XXXVIII

With Nepolian's headlight as the only source of illumination on the way, I reached Christo's house. I opened the padlocked gate with the key I had, entered, and made *him* stand on both legs. Christo wasn't there, and as a by-product of that, the whole compound was dark. The only small dull light in the compound was the park light and the tail light of Nepolian. With the help of my phone flashlight, I found the switches and turned the veranda lights on.

As I said earlier, I only had the keys to his compound gate, so I asked him for the house key. 'Under the flower pot, left side!' was his reply, but what I forgot to clarify was on whose left side; mine or the house's. Anyway, I got it on the third try.

I got in the house, turned the lights on, and for some reason, I felt the space was like home. I unmounted all my armor and bags and kept them in the room that I usually use. Since I was the only soul in the home, I roamed in minimal clothes.

The sun had tired me badly, and all I wanted to do for the rest of the day was to take a bath and sleep. I wanted cold water to bathe but ended up rinsing in warm. Food wasn't much important. The next thing was to wait for him.

His one hour had passed two hours ago, and it started to become a burden to me.

I ate a little of the leftover food I had and waited for some time, hoping he would bring something heavy to eat. My eyes stopped cooperating. I could feel the redness in my eyes, and my eyelids were closing by themselves. So to rest my eyes, I went to the room, turned the lights off, closed my eyes, and sat on the bed. My eyes started feeling relaxed, but my body also wanted a small relaxation, so I lay on the bed with my eyes closed, praying somehow to get my bag back.

XXXIX

1:50

Remembering him, I abruptly dodged out of bed and turned on the lights to check my phone. My phone showed 01:52 AM and '**14 missed calls**' from him. I didn't call back because I purposely left the main door unlocked so he could get in even if I dozed off. I heard the TV running in the hall and saw him lying on the sofa with a special sound effect: snoring. I turned the TV off, making the hall dark, and went back to catch my sleep as quickly as possible.

After ten minutes, I understood my body was charged. I went into the kitchen to see if there was anything left from his dinner, but there was nothing in the kitchen or anything interesting for me in the refrigerator. But I found my share of food on the dining table. I relieved my appetite and got into the room. Not even a single strand of sleep was floating in me to pull tight and sleep. I lay on the bed, without any thoughts; like a dead person. The loss of work was something that depressed me. I wasn't willing to share it with anyone. 'So I've to pretend like everything was fine!' I reminded myself.

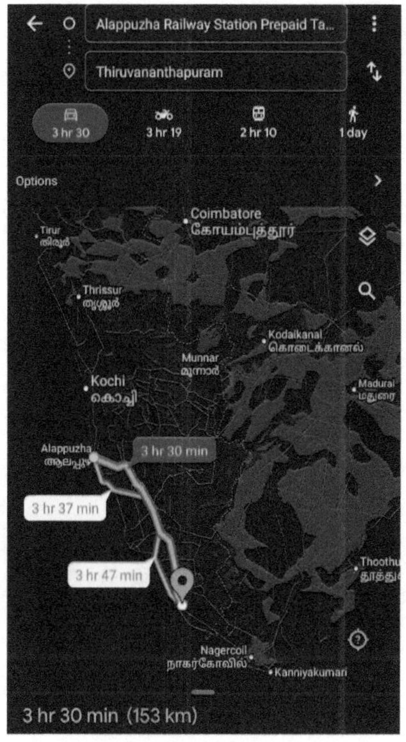

Alappuzha to Thiruvananthapuram

December 22nd, 2021

XL

We both woke up on our own time. I didn't know when he woke up, but when I completed wiping dust off Nepolian, he was on a call on the terrace. We went out for breakfast (actually, we had it at one p.m., so technically it was brunch). After washing my clothes, I lay down for some time because the previous day's sun hangover was still on me and resulted in sleeping for four hours. As I woke up, we both came up with a plan to go to a temple in the late evening, my personal favourite or maybe was; Aazhimala Shiva temple.

XLI

17:20

'*The presence of people will be less at night,*' was what I thought, and the outcome was utterly opposite. We didn't want to enter the temple due to the rush. So we went to the beach, which was at the foot of the temple. And I had a favourite spot on the rocky side of the beach.

The ambience was perfect for me, and I found the spot after so many encounters. The spot had a little rocky shade with the audible sound of waves hitting the greeny-meshy rocks, and the bubbled-up saltwater draining and joining the sea was calm to watch, and the splash made a drizzling taste of the sea.

Now the beach area had cops who didn't allow us to go near that area. I told one of the cops that 'just for sitting and enjoying the sea I came,' but he didn't let us, so I even lied that 'I came all the way from Bangalore to visit this place and temple,' but he was strong in his defence (can't blame him, some had committed suicides there recently, and this was the aftereffect of that). So we entered the temple premises, ignoring all the crowd there.

I waited and watched the big orange sun lowering into the sea.

As I said, the temple was crowded, all the credit went to the Shiva statue. I still remember the days when the statue work was going on; the number of people visiting at that time was less than fifty or so, and on Mondays and Fridays maybe between fifty to sixty, that was it. Now the number had rocketed up to almost five hundred people per day, and to be honest, ninety nine percent of the people came to take selfies with the Shiva statue, and the rest zero point one percent were the workers there, temple priests, cleaning staff, and temple committee members. They see the statue on a regular basis.

When I said five hundred people, you thought it might be for the devotion to Lord Shiva, didn't you?

Well, it's not for that; it's for the social media uploads.

I sat perpendicular to the statue. Meanwhile, he went to pray to all the Gods there. The absence of the sun in the sky resulted in turning the lights on, especially the lights that are pointed and focused towards the statue, and that's when the night beauty of the Aazhimala Shiva statue radiated.

The peak time had arrived, and the number of selfies taken doubled. The light arrangement made the area yellowish bright, making the camera capture the human face and the grey statue clearly. The sudden hike in camera usage reminded me of the pre-corona era. When the statue was under construction, people came over for praying and other devoted practices; not stretching their hands and capturing their reflections.

Before the pandemic, there was an era where we used to be more real, we talked real, we gathered, and we spent time in real as well. Now, everything has changed. Especially when the phone screen had become a must-go place for happiness, to be in touch with people, escape from loneliness, follow celebrities, and seek pleasure. The problem that it causes the most is the attention span; people lose their attention span, and day by day, it's getting reduced and causing psychological disorders. Before, we could focus on things, and now it had become really short-term; due to the vast endless less-than-a-minute videos on social media in the name of Shorts, Reels, and TikTok, our brain got addicted to these short-term dopamine rewards. Due to this, depression has skyrocketed along with suicidal provoking and existential crises in humans.

Technologically evolving is necessary and efficient, but being addicted to it and changing the well-being is not. The changes are immense. Before, there was this patience in everyone, which made the magical feel and gravity to it. Now that it has gone, everyone is in a hurry. They want at least waiting time, which makes the need lighter and short-term.

The trends have changed, making the specific age group busy in the good-for-nothing-short-term-instant-trends. Before, the dopamine hit were the things we achieve in the real world (which includes materialistic things), and now it depends on the number of likes, comments, and account followers count. In short, our social media accounts control our dopamine.

This evolution has made us humans reach everything at our fingertips, which in my perspective, is not a good evolution in the long run.

"Those times had changed, Dan," he said, sitting beside me, "now people came for the Shiva statue."

"Yeah!" I replied with visual evidence in front, "By the way, is the deity swayambhu5?" I asked.

"No, why do you ask?"

XLII

19:40

Two owls on top of the statue hijacked my attention from the rudraksha mala of the statue.

"Christo! Look, two white owls."

"Yeah, I saw," he said in a pale tone, "they have been there for a long time, did you just see them now?"

"Haa!" I grunted.

The inner part of the temple started to get rushed. The inner part is divided into two: one for the praying area with Gods' idols and the other for the Shiva statue. This is separated by metal railings, and the statue part had all the rush while the God part was kind of empty. People first go to the idol part, the majority do a formality of praying, and then get into the statue part. Solo selfies, couple selfies, family pictures, friends' pictures, kids' pictures, statue pictures, group pictures, pictures, pictures, pictures, and that ruined the traditional stance of the temple.

Dear reader, if you ever get a chance to visit the Azhimala Shiva temple, I have a request: spend some time truly observing the statue. Notice how Shiva gazes at the sky, the placement of his four hands, his dreadlocks or hair that seem to wave in the wind, the long trishula, his skull and rudraksha malas, his muscles, his fingers—essentially, take in the entire statue.

Everything about the statue is very realistic, and it is hard for anyone not to appreciate the young artist who carved it out6.

XLIII

21:30

After having our dinner, Kerala's own porotta and beef (it's not just food, it's an emotion), he got a call and got busy with it. I went towards Nepolian because I got some time to myself. I opened the toolbox, took the wiping cloth out, and started wiping the dust off. Both the mudguards, chassis, toolboxes, petrol tank, skull, fork pipe, and air filter cover are the painted parts on my Nepolian, and the rest are the unpainted parts, and that's where I was wiping.

Wiping the painted parts every day can make scratches and swirls on the paint, which eventually results in dulling the paint, which I'm allergic to. The main task is the wheels because the hubs are vintage model; cycle hubs. The brakes are not efficient, but we use engine braking as well to get the maximum braking from the bike.

Remember in chapter twelve where I did engine braking along with both the brakes while following him? If this was in normal drum brakes, I could've stopped with just any one brake in that below sixty kilometre per hour speed; more efficient, safe, and least risky when compared to cycle hubs7.

Cycle hubs have a unique feature—the spokes on both sides are lengthwise different; one side is short, and the other is long. When it comes to cleaning, it has a different story, and fingers getting stuck between the spokes are very common. So it's a hell of patience to be owned while doing it, but when all the dust is gone, it shines, and that's where the satisfaction kicks in.

December 25th, 2021

XLIV

21:00

Merry Christmas readers!

XLV

23:45

The past few days were tough for me; my Christmas was doomed. All my thoughts compressed me. I spent all the time in the room trying to find one way or the other to compensate for the lost manuscript, but nothing came to my mind.

There is a saying, 'Everything happens for a reason!' but this is one of those scenarios in my life where I have no clue what the reason was.

Now I am lying on the bed with my bags packed and Nepolian tidy. I haven't fully overcome the pain, but I have exhausted some of the frustration in the gym.

Today I've submitted the first book in my Nepolian series: '*Finally on my Nepolian*' to my publishers; in a week, it will get published. The second book in the series was what went missing. This is the third book: '*A Lost Nepolian Diary*'.

With a final check on my four a.m. alarm, I lay on the bed with my fingers interlocked on my chest and blankly

Embarked on a journey to fill the emptiness, only to find myself lost in the shadows!

GLOSSARY

Gandhiji - Slang we use for Indian rupee.

ENDNOTE

1. Old Enfields produce bass-thump sound when compared to the post-2009 manufactured ones.

2. Big billboard advertisements with flashy colours and outstanding discount offers need to be avoided on highway sides. These billboards are a distraction from the roads and need to be taken down.

3. Mahout is a person who takes care of, rides, and controls a tamed elephant.

4. The speedometer cable tends to cut off easily if the set is on the rear wheel and that's the reason why the company changed to the front wheel.

5. Swayambhu is a Sanskrit term meaning "self-manifested," "self-existing," or "that which is created by its own accord." It often refers to deities or images that are believed to have arisen naturally, without human intervention.

6. P. S. Devadathan is a talented sculptor from Azhimala, Kerala. He is best known for creating the impressive 58-foot-tall Gangadhareshwara statue at the Azhimala Shiva Temple. Devadathan started working on the statue when he was 23 years old and completed it over six years.

7. This was literally nothing, there were two close calls on

Nepolian where I got saved because of my luck not with the brakes.

ACKNOWLEDGEMENTS

I want to thank everyone who helped directly and indirectly in the whole process of completing the book.

Special thanks to,

Anushma, Goutham and Priyanka in typing the manuscript.

Akshay for proofreading.

Godfrey Selvanesan in editing the book.

PICTURES

Bridge scene mentioned in chapter-19

Lord Shiva statue in Azhimala Shiva temple

Author's Note

Hai, reader! I hope you enjoyed 'A *Lost Napoleon Diary*'. Among all my books, this is the only one that didn't go as planned—I was compelled to compromise and adapt to the book's natural flow. It took me three years to complete and publish.

Writing this book was not a pleasant experience for me. Time and again, I considered keeping it as an unpublished work. I held onto hope that I might regain my initial vision, but I soon realized that would be a waste of time.

From Chapter 23 onward, my well-being was far from peaceful, despite how I described it in the book—it was, in truth, a complete disaster. I wrote the remaining part after recovering from the trauma. Originally, the book's major events were meant to take place after reaching Thiruvananthapuram. However, due to my mental and emotional deterioration, I had to give up and conclude the story earlier than planned.

The only reason I managed to complete and publish this book was that it became an unforgettable experience in my writing career.

Thank you!

ABOUT THE AUTHOR

Dorian Snowden is an Indian author writing exclusively in English, known for narratives that blur genre boundaries and tackle themes with fearless originality. His novel *Intruder*—the first in the gripping 'Derick Abraham thriller'—was shortlisted for the 2025 Kendra Sahitya Akademi Yuva Puraskar, marking him as one of India's most exciting literary voices to watch.

Beyond the page, Dorian brings equal parts precision and passion to everything he does. With a Bachelor's degree in Pharmacy, he also holds the distinction of being Asia's youngest national bodybuilding judge, and currently serves as Vice President of the Indian Body Building Federation (IBBF), Haryana. His journey is a rare blend of creative depth and disciplined leadership—a testament to what can happen when vision meets grit.

Say connected..
Instagram: author_dorian_snowden

Also in this series:-

Finally on my Nepolian

The trip of a lifetime. A journey of exploration. Travel
across the states of India with Dorian and Goutham, and
make lasting memories. There was once a time when travel
faced restrictions—and this adventure begins in that era.
Stay with them as they overcome obstacles and continue
their motorcycle ride.

The mellifluous current of rational thought conveyed in
this book carries a gravity that compels readers to close its
pages and reflect in moments of solitude.

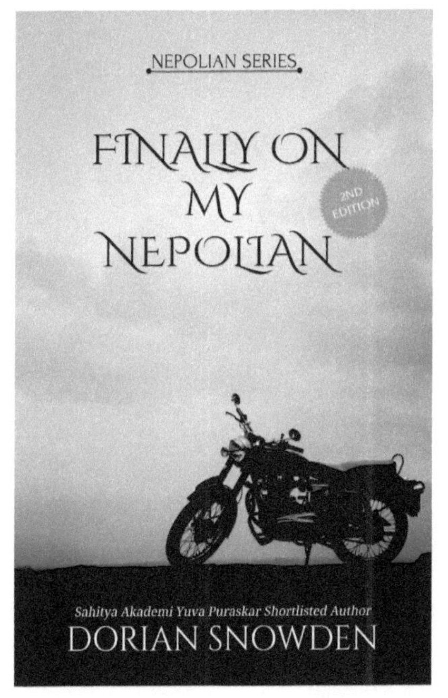

Read on for an extract....

I

17:50

He reached the front of the compound, honked twice, and walked in, opening the compound gate. I made him bring the bike inside the compound. Wearing a tan-coloured leather jacket, an SMK red-blue-white helmet, denim sky-blue pants, and a backpack, he entered.

He side-standed the 350cc Enfield, which had only one mirror, the right one—the bullet on which we were about to travel for the next couple of days. It was a 350cc Royal Enfield Stormrider sand version. The mode of transport changed from a four-wheeler to a two-wheeler due to just the two of us and a lack of Gandhiji.

With my rucksack on my back, one backpack with my laptop and other gadgets kept in the middle, and his backpack kept on the tank, both for pillion comfort and to block wind blasts onto his chest. With a full-sleeve sweatshirt on my shoulders, the sleeves gently knotted around my neck, and our helmets buckled up, we started our ride.

As we reached the front of Padmanabhaswamy Temple, we stopped and took a few pictures because uploading pictures on social media while on rides had become a norm these days.

II

No, the ride was not as good as I thought it would be; seriously!

As the ride started, the excitement and joy of exploration were overflowing through my veins. However, the moment my back started to hurt and my lower body froze due to the bike's vibration, all my overflowing energy dwindled. There were no luggage-holding back rails on the bike, only the stock grab rail, which made me carry the entire rucksack's weight on my shoulder without any support.

The weather was surprisingly okay when we started our ride. We had initially scheduled the ride for three days earlier, on October 31st. Unfortunately, three to four Covid cases were reported near where I stayed, which turned out to be Covid-negative. It had rained a few days before, and these people got wet and caught colds, planting the seed of fear—Covid-19. What should have been cleared in two days with hot beverages and food ended up causing other physical illnesses and fear in the entire area.

Personally, I was not at all concerned about this corona thing happening near me. However, according to the media, Thiruvananthapuram had the highest corona rate, and Goutham had a logical reason. 'Just because you don't believe in this doesn't mean everybody shouldn't. People in different districts will have unpleasant feelings about us, and guess what, even if someone has a common cold, there will be people making it out to be Covid-19, and the blame will be on us. Just like how a guy came from Italy, visited three hundred houses in three days, and froze the entire Kerala.' I supported his statement. But the logical thing I didn't understand was, 'We started our ride hardly four days after that fake corona incident, and won't people think the same even if we had started after two weeks? No matter what, we are human beings, and we have the tendency to blame others, even if the mistake was ours (no offense)'.

In between, we faced mild rain with lightning. Thunder and wind were comparatively lower with lightning. Goutham knew the route by heart, so checking Google Maps was not necessary until Kochi. Both of our phones were kept in my backpack along with the laptop, which I kept in the middle. The sweatshirt that I tied around my neck was covering the backpack from the top.

After thirty to forty-five minutes of riding in the rain, we decided to pull over just to stretch. The first thing I did was check whether the bag got wet. The sweatshirt worked as I expected—not even a teeny-tiny drop of water on the bag. Our pants and shoes got soaked in the rain, and my trapezius was so tired that when I tried to carry the laptop backpack, my shoulders weren't cooperating with me. That's when he came up with the plan of keeping the rucksack on the petrol tank and me wearing his backpack. That was indeed a good idea, but we wondered why we didn't think of it in the first place.

Placing the rucksack horizontally with the gadget bag in the middle, the sweatshirt properly covered, and his backpack on my shoulder, we rolled on.

III

21:30

The next stretch was at Alappuzha, between nine-thirty and ten p.m. We saw an empty hotel on the highway side, and it looked clean as well.

We stopped the bike in front and got down. The owner was alone—no suppliers, no customers, just us—and I didn't feel there would be any food by the ambiance. He indicated for us to get in. We ordered porotta and black chickpeas curry for each of us.

I have a strict rule of 'don't waste food!' and Goutham was about to leave half the curry as leftovers. He didn't say anything when I asked, "Why are you wasting food?" Without asking again or thinking twice, I took the curry saucer and poured it onto my plate.

The owner became so friendly with us, and just as we were about to finish, we ordered tea. Usually, after nine p.m. it's hard to get tea. Some places have it, and some don't. Until he asked, we thought there wasn't any, because the tea-making stands weren't at the entrance, which usually indicates the availability of tea.

Dark rainy clouds hung in the sky, a cold breeze blew just before the rain, and a cup of hot tea—those who have experienced it will understand that feeling. But the way the tea was served disappointed me; it was in a disposable paper cup. The moment when the waiter brings the tea in a glass cup and places it in front of us, making a little sound as it touches the table, it's like saying "cheers". The bubbles on top and the fumes rising between the bubbles can't be experienced with the paper cup version. This corona situation screwed that up as well. More than that, the visual feel I get when I look at the transparent glass with the tea, and with every sip, the bubbles lowering along with the tea, is incomparable to some stupid drawings on the paper cup.

While he was busy checking the views on his status, I was busy with the U.S. election, Trump-Biden (even though I knew who would win).

Goutham called his brother to stay awake. He didn't say that we were going there, but to say something important. He promised he would stay awake. Without any further discussion, we started again with wet pants and shoes, and our bags placed just as they were when we arrived.

ALL BOOKS BY DORIAN SNOWDEN,

DERICK ABRAHAM SERIES

NEPOLIAN SERIES

DECEPTION SERIES

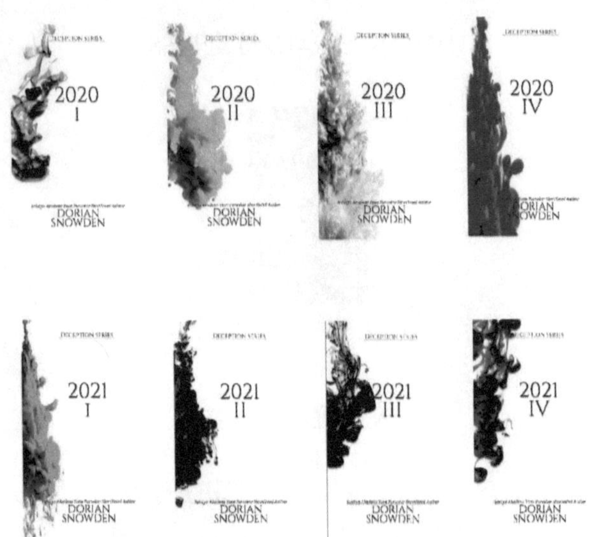

NOVELLA

www.ingramcontent.com/pod-product-compliance
Lightning Source LLC
Chambersburg PA
CBHW020541160726
47991CB00002B/535